The Beauty in All

josehess.com

The Beauty in All

Observations by

JOSE HESS

America's Award-Winning Jewelry Designer

JOSE & MAGDALENA HESS

HESS press

Dedication

"Look at that beautiful Moon." We always enjoyed the magical moon and its phases. Jose would always sing to our son, Josef, "Mira mira la lunita, mirala como se rie mirala que linda esta," a Spanish song which speaks of the beautiful moon smiling at us.

This was Jose's spirit, to see *the beauty in all*—a rose petal with a drop of dew, a tree branch glowing in the sun. He used these inspirations in life to design, to create, and to bring those visions into his works of art.

Jose's reflections, his views on so many of life's moments and life's journeys, are written here.

This book is dedicated to my precious husband Jose Hess. Thank you for all your love, for the gift of our son Josef, and for giving us your heart.

We are forever blessed.

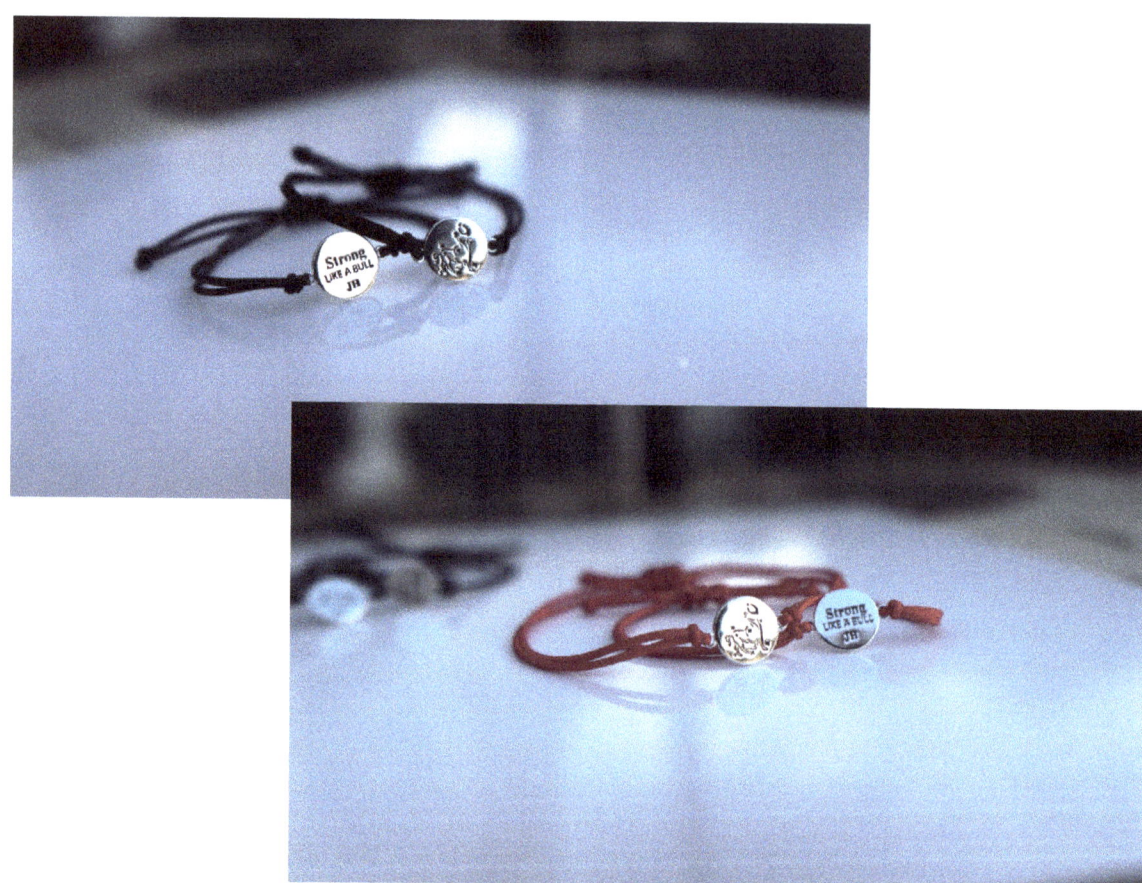

"As you venture through your life
lift your head high
stand in your beautiful power
and walk with courage, confidence and positivity
and be strong like a bull."

—Jose Hess

Contents

Preface

People often ask, "How do you come about creating your designs, tap into your creative mind, *how how how?*"

Jose Hess often answered, in his simple way, "It's a flower, it's the morning rising sun, it's all love."

But everyone always wanted to hear more. He sat one day and thought of his life's journeys, his history, his present, and how he viewed and lived this beautiful life.

I am blessed to have had Jose as soulmate, creative partner, friend, husband, and the love of my life.

I am blessed to have our son Josef who reminds me every day of Jose, his values, and his passions. This book is for you.

And this book is for all family and friends in our lives.

May you walk with a smile, and may you see the beauty in all.

Love,

Magdalena Hess

Love

The most difficult word of all, *love* can mean so many different things. Love is something that no human being can be fully happy without. There is the love of a parent, a brother, friend, or an animal. Each has different degrees of intensity.

Love given is not always returned in the same way. But if one truthfully loves, no measurement should be taken. Affection should be given freely, not demanding return.

Then there is the love of work, music, art, or nature—things more abstract where no return exists except that which is taken. In whichever way one participates, this type of love is most fulfilling because you can control that which you take and feel its richness. It is important to recognize these things so they can be part of life.

Then there is romantic love. This is accompanied by so many feelings, most beyond description. Falling in love can't be planned or hunted for, it just happens when you least expect it. It brings with it much joy and at the same time, fear, passion, and tenderness. All of these are part of being in love, and if understood and balanced, can bring the experience of heights beyond imagination.

We sometimes mistake being in love with liking someone because of their character or because of physical attraction, but I believe really being in love means that person is so important to you, your own needs take second place and you want to become *part* of that person. It means you are *friends* yet with passion, eager for their touch and closeness, and sharing your emotions with the whole person.

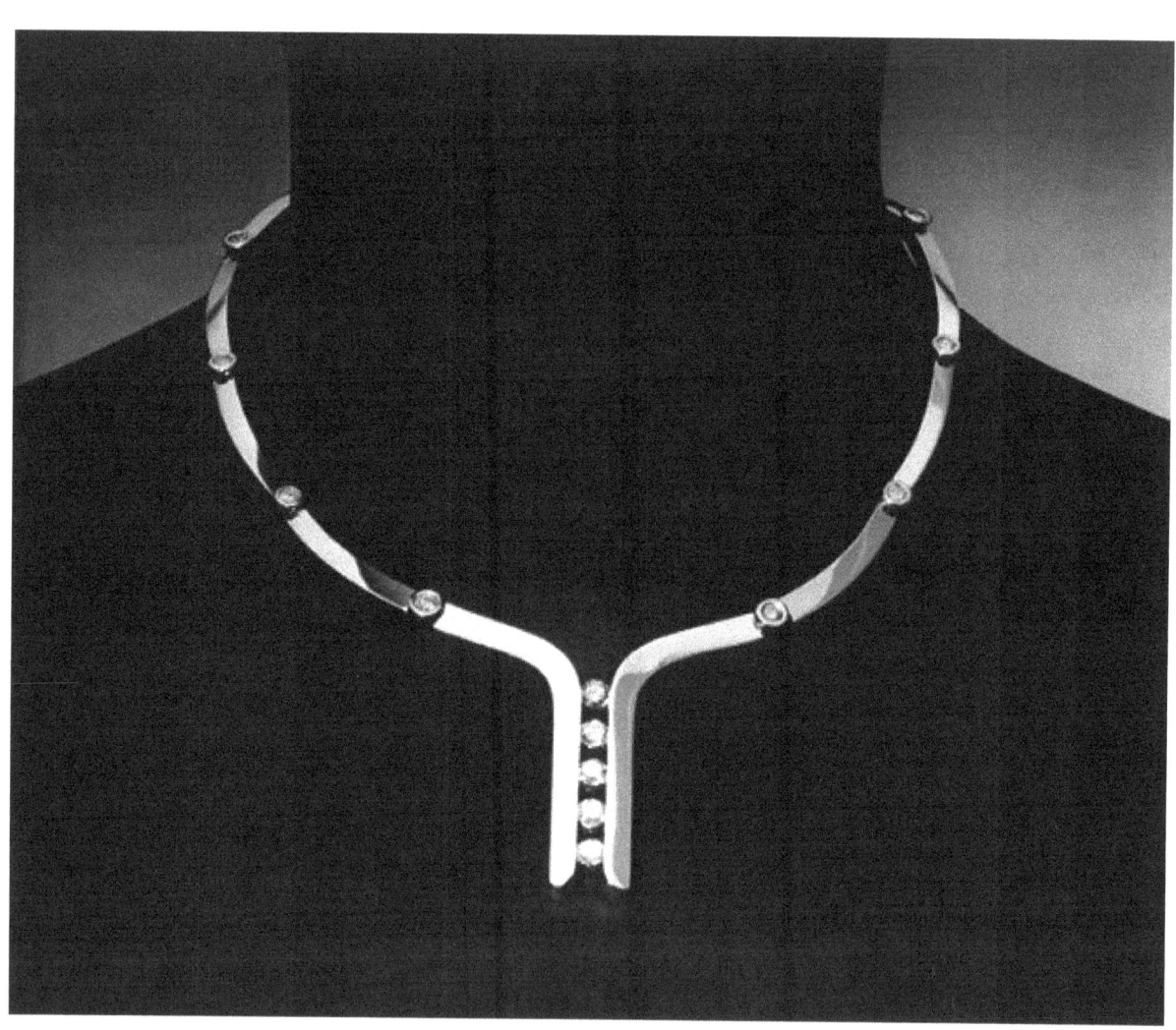

Beauty

What a difficult thing to define! Most people go through life not understanding that beauty is all around us, and we need only open our minds and our eyes to it.

It can be a sunset or the wind blowing in someone's hair.

People are the most fascinating to watch. I wish we would all learn to understand these things and have enough sensitivity to reach for them, the things human beings create with their hands and minds—paintings, sculptures, so many different objects, shapes, colors, sounds.

Life can be so full and so simple. One must learn not to demand too much but to appreciate simplicity. The biggest fault is to always want more, better, bigger, instead of being content with something natural and simple.

I remember many years ago I was having dinner with a very good friend in St. Thomas. We went to a rustic restaurant by the sea from where you could watch the waves splashing against huge rocks. During dinner I commented on what a nice place she had taken me to, and how great it all was, "but wouldn't it be nice if they had some background music?"

"Why?" she asked. "Isn't the sound of the sea enough?"

I never forgot those words and their meaning.

Humor

What a wonderful thing! To be able to laugh at some of life's problems and difficulties is a relief from their tensions. Things don't always have to be taken seriously, or they become boring.

The best kind of humor to me is that which comes spontaneously.

Humor can be a way of showing your warmth and affection. Humor can also make intolerable working situations passable. One should not be embarrassed to enjoy a good laugh. On the contrary, the looser you are with humor the more well-liked you will be.

A bright big smile on your face is priceless!

LOVESAVER SALVAMOR SAUVEUR AMOURETTE LIEBESRETTER SALVAMORE サ ラブセーバー

Hate

There is no room in my life for hate. There is so much to do, to enjoy, that wasting your energy with hate is an ugly, useless feeling which doesn't make any sense.

Obviously, we can't always agree with all people, and there are times when someone does something terrible to you.

I try to discard negative feelings. If I am hurt by someone, I try to solve the problem if I can, or I forget it and go on with something else. I try not to carry anger within me. This can make someone bitter and unpleasant.

Selfishness

It's so common and so easy to be selfish, sometimes without realizing it. In today's fast-paced world, it is often easy to think only of our own needs without regard to those around us.

One should sometimes pause and reflect on what is important to the loved ones around us and see if we can help them quietly, whether it be a physical or emotional thing. It's very important to have an awareness of those we love and a caring eye, even for those strangers who cross our path. Simple courtesy is essential because we then feel good about our actions, and others feel good about us.

Sometimes it's necessary to sacrifice a small pleasure of our own to provide a good moment for a person we care about.

Friendship

We sometimes mistake the meaning of this word. So many times, I hear someone say about a person they hardly know, "He is a very good friend of mine."

I would prefer to say, "I know them," or, "I know them very well." I don't like to use the word *friend* unless the person is close and sincere with me, and I feel the same about them.

Life teaches us, unfortunately, that many who call themselves your friends can turn their backs on you easily when you are in need of their help.

If you are lucky to have a true friendship, cultivate it, because it's a precious rarity.

Work

Some people think of work as an unpleasant thing, but I believe any work can be made pleasant and rewarding; that if one has a dull job, with enthusiasm and interest one can turn that job into something more, and when your progress is recognized, usually you are offered an opportunity for something better. People who succeed usually do it that way. Sometimes you must begin with an uninteresting activity and work your way up.

It's hard to understand not giving one's best at work, whether at a job or at home. It could so easily be creative.

My own work is a source of pleasure to me. I do not feel that just because I work long hours I am trapped. On the contrary, it is a rewarding thing to watch my own progress, and to see myself grow as an artist and as a person.

There may be times when your work seems to overshadow your relationship(s). Your partner or friends can feel jealous or resentful, or feel your activity takes you away from them. These feelings are natural, but if you let these feelings go unaddressed, you may create a wall between you.

A person must be able to work and grow, free to fully enjoy what they do.

Discretion

Privacy is one of the most important things to me. I respect it in others, and I expect the same from others.

If I observe something concerning others which might be embarrassing to them if related, I keep it to myself and mention it to no one when told something in confidence that is sacred.

Money

This is not one of the most important things for me—It's not that I don't enjoy using money to buy the things that give me pleasure and to provide what my family needs, but money for its own sake, its accumulation, is not of value to me.

So the question arises, "Why work for it, then?" The answers are simple: First, money is to provide for our daily needs. Second, money can be a measurement of success.

If one is able through their work to be well-paid, it is a reward for something done well. Usually, the better you are at something, the more money you will make. If looked at in this way, money can be fun and not an obsession.

If you have sufficient money you should also be generous enough to know how to share your good fortune. If one is aware of a fellow man's problem and able to make some contribution for betterment, how can one be indifferent? Unfortunately, we have not yet all learned this lesson, the result being enmity among individuals and war between countries.

Careful measurement should be taken so that one's actions in order to acquire money will not cause someone harm.

Raising Children

We all want our children to experience every aspect of living to the fullest, and this can be a monumental task. Helping children understand this is for their benefit, even if unrecognized presently, is not always easy.

Age makes a big difference. It is only in later years that all the things they rebelled against start to make some sense.

There is often a big temptation for a parent to give in to a child's wishes when there is particular resistance by the child to do something being asked of them, because the child feels it is not necessary. I strongly feel that not insisting, and letting the child have his own way, will make peace at the moment, but is a betrayal of one's duty as a parent, and a disservice to the child.

Once the child enters adulthood, the parent has to learn to no longer dictate or demand, but simply be a friend and someone who a child can relate to on an equal basis.

Affection

Many people are reluctant to show affection, not only to those close to them, but in general. I assume it is shyness, or fear of ridicule, or rejection.

How sad not to be able to demonstrate how one feels; how beautiful to watch people embrace in greeting.

Freedom

Philosopher Jose Marti once said, "The only thing man has that's really free, and no one can touch nor take away, is his mind."

The freedom to think, and to be respected for that, is extremely important to me.

I feel that we all have the complete right to our own point of view and should not be expected to change those views to please someone who disagrees.

I have an open mind to all thoughts and respect everyone's right to that.

This is an extremely important factor to me. If you try to change someone's views by conversation, it is acceptable, but when you demand a change, that becomes a break of respect. I feel we should not try to rule someone else's emotions.

Living

The everyday happenings, small things that occur to us, can all be made meaningful by our involvement. To notice the birthday of someone you work with even with a small gesture, to dance at someone's wedding, or participating somehow in their joy, adds meaning.

If someone is singing folk songs, clap your hands! Or send a funny card to a friend, even if it is not their birthday. Why not?

It is so important not to become a spectator in life but to participate and share, to be curious and unashamed to feel.

Marriage

Marriage is one of the most important steps in life. It determines the style in which one will live and possibly the children to be.

For some this is the natural step to take after one falls in love.

I feel what I shared about love and friendship and mutual respect from one another's freedom of mind, will make a marriage work.

Each partner should keep alive the little humorous things they share, and once in a while, do the unexpected, crazy little things that make living so much fun.

It is important to pay complete attention to the marriage and each other from all aspects, and to love fully.

The Wind Beneath My Wings

Written as part of a speech given by Jose.
Pin designed by Jose for Magdalena and engraved.

There is a very special person in this room I would like to recognize. For those of you who don't know her, she is Maggie Hess, my wife.

Maggie has been a great influence in my life, and has taught me many things. Above all, she is a constant reminder to me that the simple things in life are the most beautiful. The smell of a flower, the glow of a candle in the evening. She is as beautiful inside as she is outside.

She is the wind beneath my wings.

About the Authors

JOSE HESS dedicated the majority of his life to his passion for jewelry design, a journey that stems back to his early teens when he worked as a goldsmith's apprentice. His adoration for the art form was born, and following a desire to learn more, he studied at the Gemological Institute of America and the Mechanics Institute of New York, where he ultimately earned his Jewelry Design Degree.

Hess' professional accomplishments include numerous prestigious awards. He served as president of both The Manufacturing Jewelers and Suppliers of America, and the was the first American elected-president of the World Jewelry Confederation (CIBJO). He is a founding member of the American Jewelry Design Council.

Additionally, the designer has shared his wealth of knowledge with students as an instructor at New York's acclaimed Fashion Institute of Technology.

About the Authors

MAGDALENA HESS

is an award-winning jewelry designer and philanthropist. She describes her passion for jewelry as an opportunity to tell stories through her designs. With over four decades in the jewelry industry, she says, "Creating products that are meant to enrich people's lives is so extraordinarily rewarding."

Educated at the Gemological Institute of America, Hess spent most of her career as creative partner at Jose Hess Design working side-by-side with her multi-award-winning designer husband, Jose Hess. She has traveled the world acquiring knowledge about the international jewelry industry.

Hess served as Vice President of the Women's Jewelry Association (WJA) where she directed the organization's annual WJA Awards Gala which recognizes important women in the industry and brings together global leaders to celebrate women's talent.

Today, Magdalena continues to maintain the integrity and quality the Hess brand has become synonymous with while opening it up to a new generation concerned with timeless style.

Jose Hess Designs

SIMPLE GLAMOUR has always been a cornerstone of our designs, as exemplified by those who have worn them. Today the brand is focused on creating sophisticated simplicity with delicate pieces that can be paired with red carpet gowns as easily as with jeans and a t-shirt, making them versatile and accessible for a variety of styles.

Our jewelry is designed to be timeless. It has always been our personal belief that elegance doesn't have to be complicated, and our brand continues to hold that philosophy sacred.

We strive to ignore the constant demand for novelty, creating designs that possess an elevated character and a quality that conveys a sense of permanence. The sea, a photograph, a movie, or simply a walk in the evening can trigger creativity. We help people refine their style through our designs by following three golden rules:

Eliminate the superfluous.

Emphasize comfort.

Acknowledge the elegance of the uncomplicated.

Accomplishments & Awards

———

1963 DeBeers Diamonds International

1958-1964 Certificate of Commendation - Diamonds International Awards

1978 Certificate of Distinction, Art Direction Magazine

1978 Art Director's Club Merit Award

1978 DeBeers Diamonds Today

1981 Chicago Jewelry Show - Best in Show

1981 DeBeers Diamonds Today

1981 International Gold Corp. Certificate of Merit

1982 International Gold Corp., Certificate of Merit

1986 American Gem Trade Association Spectrum

1987 Japan Pearl Promotion Society

1988 Japan Jewelry Designers Association

1989 DeBeers Diamonds Today

1990 Pacific Jewelry Show - Best Large Exhibit

1991 DeBeers Diamonds Today

1993 Manufacturing Jewelers and Silversmiths of America - Hall of Fame

1993 DeBeers Diamonds Today

1995 DeBeers Diamonds Today

1996 DeBeers Diamonds Today

1997 Hall of Fame Award - Contemporary Design Group

Women's Jewelry Association Award

Commendation Letter from Mayor David Dinkins

Commendation Letter from Mayor Michael Bloomberg

Ronald McDonald House NYC Pediatric Cancer Housing

American Jewelry Design Council – Founding Member

Manufacturing Jewelers and Silversmiths

International Jewelry Designers Guild

Association Memberships

CIBJO (First American President of CIBJO)

DeBeers Carat Club

24 Karat Club of New York City

Plumb Club Past President

American Gem Society

Jewelry Information Center Jewelers Security Alliance

Jewelers Vigilance Committee

Press

To name a few, Maggie has been featured and quoted in several newspapers and magazines:

The Suburbanite

The Record

The Press Journal

The Bergen Health & Life for Come Laugh

Diamonds.net: "Signature Style Makes Diamonds Today"

Hess Family Philanthropy

———

Founded the non-profit organization, "Come Laugh," with a mission to bring laughter to children living with illness and adults coping with the degenerative effects of aging.

Volunteer at the Ronald McDonald House

Founded "Alpine Rocks," an educational program that taught improv comedy to kids via a workshop format that helped children develop public speaking, poise, and confidence skills.

Appendix: Advice to Aspiring Designers

Taken from a speech by Jose Hess to students.

I would like to share as much as possible of what I know about the jewelry design field in the hope that this will help you plan the direction you want to go in.

Some of you are considering jewelry design because you have a creative mind that is asking to flourish. Or, you see this as a glamorous field to make a living in. Or your family is in the jewelry business, and it's expected you will follow in their footsteps.

What is a jewelry designer? The term can be confusing. It can be someone who thinks of beautiful things and is able to put them on paper. It can also be someone who has excellent drawing skills but is not creative. This person can be very useful in a large company as an assistant designer.

Then there is the goldsmith, with the skill to translate an existing design into a finished piece of jewelry. It is possible for a Goldsmith to also have design skills, which makes them more rounded.

In large jewelry manufacturing companies, the goldsmith skills are converted to specialists. One can be a model maker or an assembler, diamond setter or polisher. This is primarily done to increase efficiency and productivity.

I would define a large company as having ten or more people working in production. If smaller than that, each craftsperson would handle more than one of the skills I just described.

As if what I have just described is not enough, a newcomer came to our industry about 25 years ago. The name ? "CAD CAM[1]." These skills, particularly CAD, revolutionized design and manufacturing as we knew it. It made the work more precise and lowered the cost of labor.

So now, as you are trying to decide whether to be a designer or goldsmith, you need to think about being a CAD operator, a skill in demand.

Or, do you want to be all these things? Tough decision.

If your intention is to work for a company, I suggest you not try to be all, but select one of these skills you like best and become very good at it, which will make you very valuable to the industry.

If you intend to start your own company, I suggest you become a designer since the jewelry needs to reflect who you are. The skills of making the product, you can hire a craftsperson for or use contractors.

So, you've decided on design, and you have learned how to draw, and it's now time to develop your first pieces. It is at this point people ask me, "How do you find ideas? How do you get Inspirations?"

---

[1] The term "CAD-CAM" is generally used to describe the software that is used for design and machining or manufacturing with a CNC Machine. CAD is an acronym for Computer Aided Design and CAM is an acronym for Computer Aided Manufacturing. CAD software is used to create things by designing and drawing, using geometric shapes to construct a model. —https://bobcad.com

There are two ways: If you love life and beautiful things, you will get ideas spontaneously without looking for them—from a cloud formation, a piece of furniture, the waves in the ocean. When that happens, you better quickly find a pencil and paper and scribble it down before you forget it.

The other way is by hard work. You start with a deliberate thought of building a collection with price points in mind, or you design for someone on request, following their wishes. This is much harder than following a spontaneous inspiration and will test your ability as a designer.

What is the most terrifying moment in a designer's life? It's morning, you are ready to start your day, you sit at your desk, and there is your pencil and an empty white sheet of paper. We all have moments like that.

Then you start, get into it, and things begin to happen. A moment will come when you really have something, and a feverish rush comes to your head, impossible to describe. Your design is now complete and the process starts all over again.

So now you have chosen what you want to do. You go to school and learn the basics. If you used your spare time wisely, you read and researched different art forms, from painting and sculpture, and read the history of the artists of earlier eras.

You are now ready to look for employment. You need to be aware that the skills you have learned so far may not be sufficient to start a business and that the best way to start is to work for an established company. This will result in starting in an entry-level position as an assistant. This is the sacrifice that needs to be made to ultimately work your way up the ladder.

More Information

For more information or to contact the authors please visit:

www.JoseHess.com

www.ingramcontent.com/pod-product-compliance
Lightning Source LLC
Chambersburg PA
CBHW041524120626

46551CB00018B/2557